BLUE AND BEAUTIFUL: PLANET EARTH, OUR HOME

BY RUTH ROCHA
AND OTAVIO ROTH

The image of our planetary home, captured most fittingly in this book, should be presented again and again so that people everywhere will come to value anew a unique, beautiful and priceless heritage.

Perhaps a good place to begin, as the author has done, is with our children. And that is why we consider this volume so timely and important. We are also encouraged by the fact that it gives a new vitality and meaning to the Stockholm Declaration on the Human Environment, which represents perhaps the first global consensus on our common responsibility for the care and maintenance of this small planet—so beautiful and so blue.

We present it with the hope for a brighter future to you, the children of the world.

Javier Pérez de Cuéllar

THIS IS THE PLANET EARTH.

THIS IS WHAT IT LOOKS LIKE FROM A LONG WAY AWAY.

BLUE AND BEAUTIFUL.

THIS IS WHERE WE LIVE,
WHERE WE HAVE ALWAYS LIVED.

AND WHERE OUR CHILDREN,
AND OUR CHILDREN'S CHILDREN
WILL HAVE TO LIVE —

FOR THERE IS ONLY ONE
EARTH.

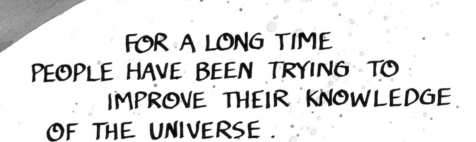

FOR A LONG TIME
PEOPLE HAVE BEEN TRYING TO
IMPROVE THEIR KNOWLEDGE
OF THE UNIVERSE.

THEY PEER THROUGH MORE AND MORE POWERFUL
TELESCOPES.
THEY BUILD ROCKETS THAT CAN TRAVEL
FURTHER AND FURTHER.

THEY PICK UP SIGNALS THROUGH MORE AND
MORE SENSITIVE ANTENNAE.

BUT NOBODY IN THE ENTIRE UNIVERSE,
HAS YET DISCOVERED A SINGLE PLANET
LIKE OURS :

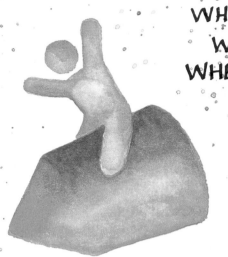

WHERE THERE IS AIR ,
WHERE THERE IS WATER ,
WHERE THERE IS LIFE !

FOR THERE IS ONLY
ONE EARTH.

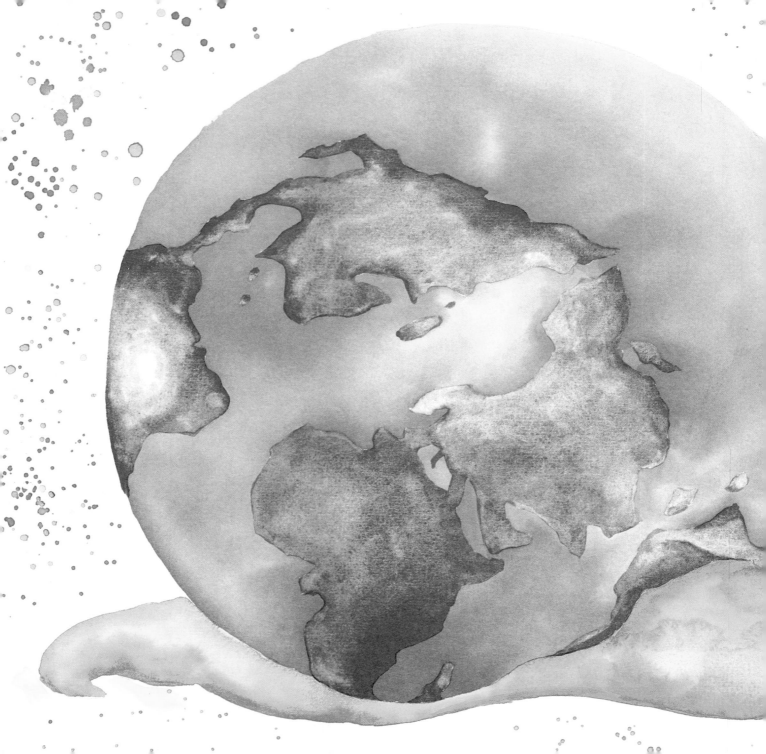

BUT IF THE EARTH IS TO CONTINUE GIVING US
EVERYTHING WE NEED
TO STAY ALIVE,
WE WILL HAVE TO TAKE VERY GOOD CARE OF IT.

JUST AS WE TAKE CARE
OF OUR HOMES.
EVEN BETTER, IN FACT.

BECAUSE WE CAN ALWAYS
MOVE TO A NEW HOME.

BUT WE CANNOT MOVE
TO A NEW PLANET.

AND AT THIS MOMENT,
WE ARE NOT TREATING
THE EARTH
AS CAREFULLY AS WE
SHOULD BE.

THIS IS WHY THE COUNTRIES
THAT BELONG TO THE
UNITED NATIONS
ARE WORRIED ABOUT WHAT IS
HAPPENING TO THE
ENVIRONMENT.

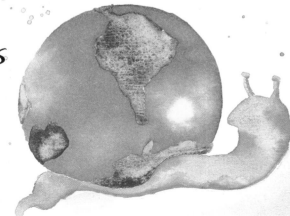

THEY HAVE HELD MEETINGS
        TO DECIDE WHAT TO DO ABOUT IT.

    AT THESE MEETINGS,
        THEY HAVE DRAWN UP DECLARATIONS,
ACTION PLANS, PRINCIPLES AND GUIDELINES
    — SETTING OUT WHAT CAN BE DONE
        TO ENSURE THAT THE EARTH —
            — OUR HOME —
        DOES NOT BECOME A HOSTILE PLACE
            WITH MANY DESERTS,
            POISONED WATERS AND WITHOUT FORESTS,
WHERE IT WOULD BE VERY DIFFICULT TO LIVE.

THESE DECLARATIONS, PRINCIPLES
AND GUIDELINES
ALL HAVE THE SAME MESSAGE, AND THIS IS WHAT
IT SAYS:

ALL HUMAN BEINGS ARE EQUAL,
WITH AN EQUAL RIGHT TO A GOOD LIFE
IN A HEALTHY ENVIRONMENT.

EVERYONE HAS A DUTY TO PROTECT
THE ENVIRONMENT AND
ALL FORMS OF LIFE.

THE EARTH'S RESOURCES
— THE AIR, THE WATER, THE LAND,
THE PLANTS, AND THE ANIMALS —
HAVE TO BE PROTECTED
BECAUSE THIS IS FOR THE GOOD OF ALL
LIVING CREATURES,
AND FOR ALL CREATURES THAT WILL LIVE
ONE DAY IN THE
FUTURE.

THE WAY WE TREAT
THE EARTH —
AND THE STEPS WE TAKE
TO PROTECT IT,
HAVE TO BE VERY CAREFULLY
PLANNED.

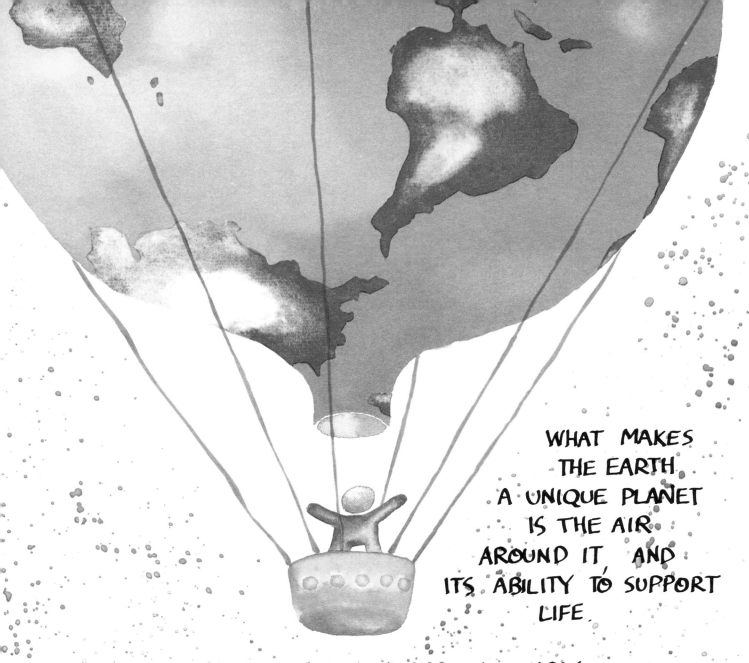

WHAT MAKES
THE EARTH
A UNIQUE PLANET
IS THE AIR
AROUND IT, AND
ITS ABILITY TO SUPPORT
LIFE.

IT IS THE ONLY PLANET, AS FAR AS WE KNOW,
WHERE LIFE IS POSSIBLE.

WE MUST ALL
    MAKE AN EFFORT TO STOP POLLUTING
THE WATERS, THE SEAS, THE RIVERS, AND THE LAKES
        THAT PROVIDE US WITH FOOD,
TRANSPORTATION, WEALTH AND LEISURE.

THE LAND IS VERY GENEROUS TO US:
IT GIVES US WOOD
AND CLAY TO BUILD OUR HOUSES,
IRON AND ALUMINIUM
TO RUN OUR INDUSTRIES,
OIL AND COAL TO GIVE US WARMTH AND
ENERGY,
AND MUCH, MUCH MORE.

MOST IMPORTANT OF ALL,
THOUGH, IS THAT
THE LAND GIVES US
OUR FOOD.

COMMON SENSE TELLS US
IT WOULD BE WRONG TO
POLLUTE THE SOURCE
OF OUR FOOD.

OUR WORLD HAS TAKEN MANY YEARS
TO BECOME WHAT IT IS TODAY.

TO DESTROY SO MUCH AS A SINGLE
SPECIES OF PLANT OR ANIMAL
UPSETS THE BALANCE OF NATURE AND
CAN CAUSE SERIOUS
CONSEQUENCES FOR THE
WHOLE HUMAN RACE.

HUMAN BEINGS HAVE TO LIVE
IN HARMONY
WITH ALL OTHER SPECIES.

WHENEVER WE INTERFERE
WITH NATURE,
WE HAVE TO BE VERY CAREFUL
OR WE RISK INJURING
OURSELVES.

WE HAVE TO MAKE SURE
WE ARE NOT DAMAGING
SOMETHING THAT TOOK MILLIONS
OF YEARS TO EVOLVE AND
BECOME LIFE-SUPPORTING.

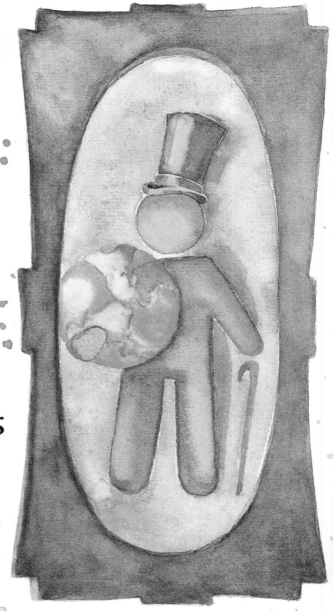

WHAT WE HAVE RECEIVED
FROM OUR ANCESTORS
WE WANT TO PASS ON TO
OUR CHILDREN
AND THEIR CHILDREN —
BUT IN A BETTER,
NOT WORSE STATE
THAN WE FOUND IT.

WE MUST PUT AN END TO POLLUTION
AND INVENT
BETTER WAYS OF LIVING –
BY SHOWING RESPECT TO ALL
LIVING CREATURES,
WITHOUT WASTE AND
WITHOUT POISONING NATURE.

IF WE CAN DO THIS WE SHALL ALL BE
HEALTHIER AND
HAPPIER
PEOPLE.

PEOPLE EVERYWHERE
WANT TO LEAD A BETTER
LIFE,
AND IT IS ONLY RIGHT THAT
THEY SHOULD.
GOVERNMENTS SHOULD
WORK TOGETHER
TO PLAN THE PROPER USE
OF THE RESOURCES
THAT BELONG TO US ALL,
BECAUSE
WE ALL LIVE
IN THE SAME HOME
—THE EARTH—
AND WHAT ONE PERSON DOES
IN ONE PART OF THE HOME
WILL AFFECT OTHERS
IN OTHER PARTS.

BY HELPING EACH OTHER, WE CAN ALL IMPROVE OUR STANDARD OF LIVING WITHOUT HARMING THE ENVIRONMENT IN THE CITIES OR IN THE COUNTRYSIDE.

ALL THE SCIENTIFIC KNOWLEDGE
        THE HUMAN RACE HAS ACCUMULATED
MUST BE PUT TO WORK
        IN THE SERVICE OF THE EARTH
— TO DISCOVER BETTER WAYS FOR US TO LIVE —
    AVOIDING ALL WASTE,
        AND COMBATING ALL FORMS
            OF POLLUTION.

    THIS MEANS WE HAVE TO PAY
            CLOSER ATTENTION TO NATURE,
        TRYING TO UNDERSTAND IT,
            AND LEARNING FROM IT,
    AND ABOVE ALL, PROTECT IT AS IT PROTECTS US.

    THEREFORE, EVERYONE MUST LEARN TO BE
            CONCERNED ABOUT THE
                ENVIRONMENT.

IT IS NECESSARY TO EDUCATE POLITICIANS,
SCIENTISTS, TEACHERS AND
EVEN OUR LEADERS.

THERE ARE LESSONS THEY CAN LEARN
FROM PEOPLE WHO
LIVE IN SIMPLICITY AND WISDOM,
IN HARMONY WITH NATURE.

ALSO,
EACH OF US SHOULD
LIVE
IN WAYS THAT
DO NOT HARM
THE EARTH
AND SHOULD SHARE
GOOD EXAMPLES
OF SUCH LIVING
WITH EACH OTHER.

ALL THE NATIONS IN THE WORLD
    MUST TAKE PROPER CARE OF WHAT
      BELONGS TO ALL THE PEOPLE
        — A LIFE-SUSTAINING EARTH —

SO THAT OUR INHERITANCE,
OUR ONLY INHERITANCE
- THE PLANET EARTH -
WILL BE SAFE FOR US,
FOR OUR CHILDREN,
AND FOR OUR CHILDREN'S CHILDREN.

AND OUR PLANET WILL SURVIVE.

IT WILL STILL BE WHAT IT IS TODAY:

BLUE AND BEAUTIFUL !

Following the success of their first book "The Universal Declaration of Human Rights: An Adaptation for Children," Ruth Rocha and Otavio Roth were commissioned by the United Nations to write another children's book based on the 1972 Stockholm Declaration on the Human Environment.

The result is "BLUE AND BEAUTIFUL: Planet Earth, our Home," which expresses the United Nations concern with one of the world's most pressing problems: Saving our environment, and the role each of us plays in this pursuit.